Rain, Hail, and Snow

Rain, Hail, and Snow

Trudi Strain Trueit

Franklin Watts
A Division of Scholastic Inc.
New York • Toronto • London • Auckland • Sydney
Mexico City • New Delhi • Hong Kong
Danbury, Connecticut

For my mom, Shirley Strain, who believed in a fourth-grade playwright and shared her dreams. And for Mrs. Zielinski, my fourth-grade teacher.

Note to readers: Definitions for words in **bold** can be found in the Glossary at the back of this book.

Photographs ©: AP/Wide World Photos: 25 (Ron Heflin), 2 (John Maniaci/Wisconsin State Journal), 5 left, 28, 29 (L.G. Patterson), 6 (Karel Prinsloo); Peter Arnold Inc.: 5 right, 44 (William Campbell), 19 (S.J. Krasemann), 30 (Leonard Lessin), 36 (Bill O'Connor), cover, 33 (Clyde H. Smith), 46 (Tischler Fotografen); Photo Researchers, NY: 22, 24 (Howie Bluestein), 42 (Leslie F. Conover), 10 (Stephen Dalton), 34 (Lowell Georgia), 40 (Margot Granitsas), 35 (Gilbert S. Grant), 12 (Tom HcHugh), 9 (J.P. Nacivet/Explorer), 38 (Thomas Nilson/JVZ/SPL), 26 (Mark A. Schneider), 45 (John Westcott/Yva Momatiuk); Tom Bean: 23; Visuals Unlimited: 18 (Gary W. Carter), 11 (John D. Cunningham), 17 (Patrick J. Endres), 20, 21 (Carlyn Galati), 15 (LINK), 8 (Mark S. Skalny), 14 (Doug Sokell).

The photograph on the cover is an extreme close-up of snowflakes. The photograph opposite the title page shows sixth-graders jumping in hail after a storm in Madison, Wisconsin.

Library of Congress Cataloging-in-Publication Data

Trueit, Trudi Strain.
    Rain, hail, and snow / Trudi Strain Trueit.
       p. cm. — (Watts Library)
    Includes bibliographical references and index.
    ISBN 0-531-11970-X (lib. bdg.)   0-531-16218-4 (pbk.)
    1. Precipitation (Meteorology)—Juvenile literature. [1. Precipitation (Meteorology)] I. Title. II. Series.
QC924.7 .T78 2002
551.57'7—dc21
                               2001024896

Contents

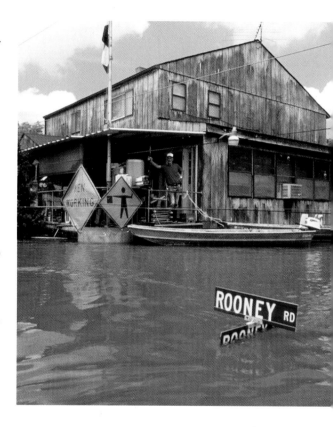

A helicopter rescues flood victims in Mozambique, where heavy rains fell for nearly two straight months in 2000.

Chapter One

The Crying Sky

Drop by drop, inch by inch, the **rains** were destroying a continent. For nearly two straight months in early 2000, dark clouds unleashed their fury on several countries in Africa. People in Mozambique watched in horror as waves of floodwaters tore through their villages, sweeping away homes and drowning valuable crops. Water supplies had become tainted and undrinkable. Diseases such as malaria and cholera were rapidly spreading through refugee camps.

Rain is crucial for all life on Earth.

Madagascar, an island off the coast of Africa, received more than 55 inches (140 centimeters) of rain during the February and March storms. Ninety percent of the nation's rice crop was destroyed. Rescuers had to fly in food and water to the 1.5 million people affected by one of the worst rains in Africa's history.

Rain is critical to the survival of life on our planet. It showers us with water to drink, nurtures crops, supports industry, and fills rivers and lakes. When we get more rain than we expect or less than we need, the fragile balance of life on Earth is threatened.

This book explores the many ways water falls on our world, from the **drizzle** that barely mists you on a foggy morning to the lacy snowflakes that you try to catch on your tongue. We will also trek through some of the most extreme weather on Earth: ice storms, hail, blizzards, and flash floods. So keep reading—and keep that umbrella handy.

Water Works

You might not be able to see it, smell it, or taste it, but water is in the air even when there is no rain or **snow**. Air-bound water takes the form of an invisible gas called **water vapor**.

Although you cannot see water vapor, you can certainly feel its effects in the air. If you have ever been sticky and sweaty on a July day, you are experiencing a high level of **humidity**, the amount of water vapor in the air.

Most **clouds** get their start when the Sun warms air containing water vapor near the ground. Since warm air is lighter than cold air, the pockets of heated air start to rise. As these air pockets, called **thermal updrafts**, rise into the atmosphere, they gradually cool. When the updrafts reach their **dewpoint**, the water vapor within them **condenses**, or turns from an invisible gas into either liquid water or ice crystals. The water molecules latch onto microscopic particles of dust, clay, soot, pollen, ocean salt, or pollutants in the air. As water condenses onto these particles—called **cloud condensation nuclei** or **CCN**—clouds begin to form.

Precipitation is any water that falls from a cloud, either as

Clouds form when water vapor condenses onto tiny particles called cloud condensation nuclei, or CCN.

Chubby Rain

By the time raindrops reach the ground, they can be anywhere from one hundred to one thousand times larger than they were inside the cloud. Still, the biggest raindrops are only about the size of a pencil eraser.

a liquid, such as drizzle or rain, or as a solid, such as snow, **sleet**, or **hail**. Precipitation occurs in two basic ways: through the warm cloud process or the cold cloud process. In the warm cloud process, the temperature remains above the freezing point of water, 32° Fahrenheit (0° Celsius). Once water vapor condenses onto CNN, the droplets in a cloud smack into one another to form larger drops. When the drops get too heavy to stay in the cloud, they fall as rain, combining on the way down to create even bigger drops. The warm cloud process always produces rain.

In the cold cloud process, below-freezing temperatures in part of the cloud create ice crystals instead of water droplets. This **freezing level** can be as low as 1,000 feet (300 meters) or higher than 20,000 feet (6,000 m). Some of the droplets inside the cloud freeze into crystals. Others never freeze at all, even though temperatures might dip well below the freezing point. These stubborn drops are called **supercooled water droplets**.

When a supercooled droplet hits a piece of ice or dust in the frozen air, it freezes onto the CCN, and an ice crystal is born. This tiny particle attracts other supercooled water droplets, and the crystal begins to grow. Once it becomes too heavy for the cloud, the crystal falls. On its way down, it collides with other crystals and clusters to form a snowflake.

If the temperature underneath the cloud is below freezing, the group of crystals will remain a snowflake. If it is above freezing, the snowflake will turn to rain. Since parts of most clouds are located in temperatures below freezing, most raindrops start out as snowflakes.

As precipitation falls, it might freeze or melt several times. This depends on how many layers of different temperatures it passes through before finally touching down. For instance, snowflakes that fall through a warm zone will melt into rain but then refreeze into sleet if they hit a pocket of cold air. What we see on the ground is only the final form of a product long in the making.

When temperatures in a cloud are below freezing, ice crystals form. If air temperatures underneath the cloud are also below freezing, the crystals combine and fall to the ground as snowflakes.

It takes at least one million cloud droplets to form one raindrop. Imagine the number of droplets it took to create this tropical rainstorm in Palenque, Mexico.

Chapter Two

Sprinkles to Showers

Most clouds never rain. In fact, only about one cloud in ten will ever part with a single raindrop. It takes at least one million (and as many as fifteen million) microscopic cloud droplets to create just one raindrop large enough to fall to Earth.

The smallest raindrops, about the size of a pinhead, are called drizzle. Drizzle happens when warm, moist air collides with slightly cooler air near the ground to produce a thick layer of low clouds.

Rain Check

Raindrops are not really shaped like tears. With their rounded tops and flat bottoms, large raindrops actually look like the tops of hamburger buns.

Although these baby drops seem harmless, a heavy drizzle can reduce visibility to less than 0.25 mile (0.5 kilometer).

Drops bigger than 0.02 inch (0.5 millimeter) are classified as rain. Raindrops rarely get bigger than 0.23 inch (6 mm), about the size of a pea—any bigger than that, and the drops are pulled apart as they plunge to Earth. Larger raindrops fall to Earth much more rapidly than smaller drops do, from 16 to 20 miles (26 to 32 km) per hour. Tiny drizzle drops can take an hour or more to fall 1 mile (1.6 km).

Some rain **evaporates**—turns from a liquid back into a gas—before it ever reaches the ground. These tiny raindrops, called **virga**, hang from beneath a cloud like white streamers

Virga look like white streamers underneath a cloud. These tiny raindrops evaporate before they reach the ground.

until they evaporate. Dry thunderstorms, such as those found in the southwestern United States, are created by virga. The lightning from these storms often triggers brush- and wildfires that quickly get out of control in the heat of the summer.

It's Raining, It's Pouring

Showers do not mean light rain, as most people think. A shower is rain that falls, sometimes quite heavily, for a short time. Showers can stop and start throughout the day between periods of blue sky. The length of a shower depends on the size of a rain cloud and how fast winds are pushing it across the sky. **Cloudbursts**, heavy rains that fall over a small area, can produce 4 inches (10 cm) of rain in less than 1 hour. In contrast, a **steady rain** is one that falls for several hours or days over an area with little or no break.

Meteorologists keep track of rainfall not only by observing the length of a storm, but also by measuring how much water comes down. As raindrops fall, they are collected in a **rain gauge**. This instrument catches water through a funnel connected to a long measuring tube. A scale inside keeps track of

A rain gauge collects water to be measured.

the amount of rainfall. The gauge can measure as little as 0.01 inch (0.25 mm) of rain. Anything less than that is considered too small to measure and is called a **trace** of rain.

Ribbons of Color

In ancient times, people used to be frightened of **rainbows**, which they believed were snakes in the sky. In African mythology, the snake brought bad luck to any home it touched. Today, of course, we know that these glowing arcs are not snakes but simply tricks of light and water.

The Sun is made up of a range of six colors: violet, blue, green, yellow, orange, and red. Shining together, these colors appear white. As sunlight passes through a raindrop, its rays are **refracted**, or bent. The light is reflected off the back of the raindrop, which separates the colors of the Sun for our

A double rainbow in Denali National Park, Alaska

eyes to see. The best time to catch a rainbow is when the Sun breaks through the clouds just after an evening storm. Keep the setting Sun to your back and look toward the rain that has just gone by.

You might also see a double rainbow, one fainter arc above the main rainbow. This happens when light inside a raindrop is reflected twice instead of once. The colors on the secondary rainbow are reversed, with violet on top and red on the bottom, as if the primary rainbow were peering into a mirror.

In the Deep Freeze

When raindrops fall through a pocket of cold air below the freezing point of water, they can freeze into ice pellets, also called sleet. Sleet is often confused with hail, since both are ice, but the two types of precipitation are created under very different conditions. Sleet develops in winter weather, while warm thunderstorms give birth to hail.

The term **freezing rain** is a bit confusing, since it is not rain that has frozen on its way down from the sky, as the name

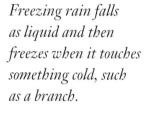

Freezing rain falls as liquid and then freezes when it touches something cold, such as a branch.

implies. Freezing rain is the term for liquid drops that freeze the moment they touch something cold. If temperatures on the ground are below freezing, the instant the rain hits the ground, it turns to **glaze**, a super-slick kind of ice.

Freezing rain, when it comes in **ice storms**, can coat a town with enough glaze to topple power lines, snap trees, and turn roads into skating rinks. The ice can even coat the wings of birds and glue the paws of dogs and cats to the ground. In the United States, the most ice-storm activity occurs in the area from Louisiana to North Carolina, where 20 to 40 percent of winter precipitation falls in the form of freezing rain.

An ice storm in Wisconsin causes a tree to snap.

19

A hail storm creates a bizarre summer scene in Tucson, Arizona.

Chapter Three

In the Path of Hail

Spring and summer thunderstorms create hail, the only kind of frozen precipitation that falls in warm weather. These chunks of ice, called hailstones even though there are no real rocks involved, can be smaller than a kernel of corn or bigger than a grapefruit. In the United States, hail causes $1 billion in crop losses and property damage each year.

Hail gets its start deep within thunderclouds in which cold and warm air collide. As moist air condenses into water

On April 14, 1986, the tiny Asian country of Bangladesh was pelted with giant hailstones. The softball-sized ice clumps killed 92 people. In 1995, grapefruit-sized hail pummeled Dallas, Texas, injuring 109 people and doing $1.2 billion in damage.

Major-League Hail

Updrafts must whip at speeds greater than 100 miles (160 km) per hour to support baseball-sized hail.

droplets, the increasing heat within the cloud causes the droplets to rise higher into the atmosphere. The droplets then freeze into ice crystals. In the cooler air, the crystals begin to fall, attracting supercooled water droplets on their way down.

Then, just as they are melting, the droplets are scooped up by a strong wind current and lifted back into the atmosphere. High in the sky, the drops freeze again, and another layer of ice forms around them. Once more the crystals fall, attract supercooled droplets, begin to melt, and are whisked back up into the sky by yet another updraft. Like a Ping-Pong ball, the hail is bounced up into the clouds again and again. Each time it goes up, another coating of ice is added, and the hailstone grows larger. Eventually, the updraft weakens, or the hailstone gets too heavy and drops to Earth.

The most common type of hail is a sphere, or ball. Hailstones also take the shape of cones, discs, stars, or irregular globes. Most hailstones are about the

Hailstones grow larger and larger as updrafts whisk them back up into the atmosphere. Here, a meteorologist holds hailstones as large as softballs.

The number of rings inside a hailstone indicates how many cycles the stone took in the sky.

size of a pea, but those that travel up into the atmosphere more than a few times become much larger. You can tell how many trips a hailstone took through the cycle by breaking it in half and counting the rings of ice inside. As many as twenty-five layers have been recorded in hailstones the size of grapefruits.

Hail Habits

Hail is most common in the middle latitudes, in such places as the Himalayas, central Europe, South Africa, southern China, India, Argentina, and the central plains of the United States and Canada. In the United States, about five thousand hailstorms hit each year. The worst hail can be found in a 700-square-mile (1,800-square-km) area that stretches from Wyoming through Colorado and Nebraska. In this region, known as Hail Alley, there are usually nine to ten days of hail per year. Often, snowplows must be called out in the summer months to clear the drifts of hail that pile up on roads.

Large, baseball-sized hailstones can dive toward Earth at speeds of more than 90 miles (145 km) per hour. Hail can crack windows, damage cars, dent airplanes in flight, and wipe out millions of dollars in crops. Falling from its dark, billowy thunderclouds, hail often resembles a hazy, white curtain. These hailstreaks usually cut a path from 300 feet (90 m) to 5 miles (8 km) long, although larger hailstreaks have been known to stretch for hundreds of miles.

Hail can be difficult to predict, but during severe thunderstorms, a green tint in the dark clouds is an indicator that hail might be brewing. This spooky glow, likely caused by ice

A White Summer

In August 1980, a storm blanketed the city of Orient, Iowa, with hail 6 feet (1.8 m) deep in places. Even in the heat of summer, it took days for all the ice to melt.

A hail-damaged car in Fort Worth, Texas

An iridescent green sky foretells the possibility of hail. This is called the green sky effect.

caught in the cycle of updrafts, is called the **green sky effect**. It is also a sign that a tornado may not be far off.

Amazing Hail Stories

The strong wind currents that churn inside thunderstorms can lift more than rain and ice into the atmosphere. These updrafts have been known to carry a few other things high into the sky. Hail victims include frogs, fish, and, on at least one occasion, a person.

In 1930, a German pilot flying in a contest to see who could reach the highest altitude was pulled into an updraft and blown 40,000 feet (12,000 m) into the air. The force of the winds broke apart his aircraft, and the pilot was carried up into a cloud, where layers of ice formed on him. He fell to his death, a human hailstone.

In 1894, a turtle fell out of the sky during a thunderstorm in Vicksburg, Mississippi. It is believed that a waterspout, a funnel cloud that comes in contact with water, flung the turtle into the atmosphere. There it became the nucleus for a giant hailstone.

Hail in History

Largest hail	Coffeyville, Kansas, 1970	Measuring 17.5 inches (44 cm) around and weighing 1.75 pounds (0.79 kilogram), a hailstone the size of a grapefruit fell to Earth.
Heaviest hail	Hyderabad, India, 1939	This hailstone weighed 7.5 pounds (3.4 kg).
Most deadly hail	New Delhi, India, 1888	Hundreds of cattle and 246 people were killed in a severe storm.
Most expensive hail	Munich, Germany, 1984	A hailstorm caused $1 billion in damage.
Most hail in the world	Kenya, Africa	On average, it hails 132 days per year.
Most unusual hail	Worcester, Massachusetts, 1933	Giant hailstones were reported to have fallen with ducks frozen inside.
Surviving hail	Dubuque, Iowa, 1882	A hailstone containing two frogs fell to the ground. When the ice melted, the frogs hopped away.
History-changing hail	Paris, France, 1788	Hail destroyed croplands in France, adding to the massive food shortage that contributed to the start of the French Revolution.

In January 1999, one of the worst snowstorms of the twentieth century struck the Midwest. By the time the raging blizzard ended, seventy-three people had died. Here, vehicles struggle to get to their destinations near Columbia, Missouri.

Chapter Four

Snowbound

On January 2, 1999, a snowstorm struck the Midwest and dumped 18.6 inches (47.2 cm) of snow on Chicago—a single-day snowfall record for that city. Along with the Windy City, the storm buried parts of Wisconsin, Indiana, and Michigan. It cut power, halted traffic, and closed airports. Thousands of travelers were stranded. More than 500,000 people were without power, some for as long as a week.

Following the blizzard, temperatures dropped to well below 0° F (-17° C), and the stage was set for an ice storm. Congerville, Illinois, hit a record-low

The Blizzard of '96 hit New York City with 20 inches (50 cm) of snow.

temperature of -36° F (-38° C). By the time it was all over, seventy-three people had died in what became one of the worst blizzards of the twentieth century.

Each year, the mainland United States is blanketed by about one hundred major snowstorms that last an average of two to five days. Rochester, New York, which typically sees about 95 inches (240 cm) of snow per year, has the honor of being the snowiest large city in the continental United States. Blue Canyon, California, near Lake Tahoe, Nevada, gets the most snow—about 240 inches (600 cm) every year.

Forming Flakes

As we have seen, snowflakes are born in the cold cloud process. Supercooled water droplets freeze onto particles in the air to become cloud condensation nuclei. When ice crystals fall from a cloud, they latch onto each other to form snowflakes. As long as the air temperature between the ground and the cloud remains below freezing, the crystals touch down as snow.

Air temperatures can wreak havoc with ice crystals to completely change their shape. **Graupel**, also called soft hail, is made of snowflakes that have fallen through a layer of supercooled water droplets. The water droplets freeze onto the flakes and coat them with a hard layer of ice called **rime**. While most graupel looks like tiny lumps of hard snow, some is shaped like ridged pyramids. Although it falls during cold weather, graupel is often mistaken for hail because the pellets bounce when they hit the ground.

Some snowflakes are made up of as many as one hundred individual ice crystals. By the time it lands, the average snowflake measures about 0.5 inch (1.3 cm) across. However, falling crystals can cling together to make flakes measuring more than 4 inches (10 cm) across.

Pancakes or Snowflakes?

On January 28, 1887, people in Fort Keough, Montana, looked up to see giant snowflakes, measuring 15 inches (38 cm) across, tumbling down.

Yellow, Maybe, but Red?

In 1755, red dust from the Sahara Desert was blown hundreds of miles north to become cloud condensation nuclei for ice crystals over Europe. The Swiss were not surprised by the early snowfall, but they were shocked to see that the snowflakes were red!

Growing a Snowflake

The typical snowflake that lands on your tongue is made up of 180 billion water molecules. There are millions of different ways these molecules can fit together, which is why you will rarely find two snowflakes that are alike. All snowflakes have one thing in common, however. Since all water molecules have six sides, every snowflake must have the same number of sides no matter how the molecules bond together: six.

In the late nineteenth and early twentieth centuries, American scientist and farmer Wilson Bentley photographed more than five thousand crystals but never came across two that were identical. For his research, Bentley caught snowflakes on a tray and flattened them out with a feather to view under his microscope. He soon began to photograph the images he saw.

Bentley identified more than eighty types of snowflakes. He believed that differences in air temperatures were responsible for shaping snowflakes in so many different patterns. Since then, scientists have learned that water content also plays a part in how crystals form. For instance, big, fluffy flakes occur when the temperature is close to 32° F (0° C). When the air is colder, there is less moisture in the crystals, so the flakes are smaller.

Today, scientists recognize seven major snowflake shapes: tubes or capped columns, stars, hexagonal plates, spatial dendrites (stars with ridged arms), hexagonal columns, needles, and irregular. High clouds, in which temperatures are well below freezing, create crystals that resemble hollow tubes or

Although many people associate star-shaped crystals with snow, this kind of flake is actually the hardest to find.

columns. Star-shaped snowflakes form in slightly higher temperatures. Mid-level clouds, where temperatures are yet higher, produce hexagonal plates that look like flattened stop signs. Low clouds, whose temperatures hover near the freezing point, offer the most moisture to growing crystals. In this layer of the sky, the most unusual and varied shapes occur: spatial dendrites, hexagonal columns, needles, bullets, plates, and columns.

Many snowflakes turn out to be combinations of plates and columns. This is because they fall through a variety of temperatures—all below 32° F (0° C)—on their way to the ground. The most common snowflake is one that has no distinct shape at all: the irregular snowflake.

Secret Ingredient

Clay is one of the most common nuclei of ice crystals. Bits of clay have been found in snowflakes in Antarctica, even though the closest source of clay dust is at the tip of South America, 2,400 miles (3,900 km) from the South Pole!

Sizing Up Snow

Meteorologists use several terms to help describe the many ways snow falls:

- **Flurry**—a light dusting of snow that will probably do no more than coat the ground in a thin white frosting
- **Snow shower**—flakes start and stop throughout the day and will likely produce enough snow to measure
- **Snowburst**—a lot of snow that falls in a very short amount of time
- **Snowsquall**—a brief but intense storm with strong winds
- **Blizzard**—a heavy snowstorm or blowing snow with winds above 35 miles (55 km) per hour and lasting at least 3 hours. A blizzard can create dangerous **whiteout** conditions, which means there is so much falling and blowing snow that you cannot tell where the ground ends and the sky begins.

This blizzard has created whiteout conditions. It is impossible to distinguish the sky from the ground.

Snow is still measured the old-fashioned way, with a ruler or yardstick. Snow pillows record the weight of snow as it accumulates. Heated rain gauges are also used to calculate snowfall by melting the water. Scientists used to figure that 10 inches (25 cm) of snow melted down to about 1 inch (2.5 cm) of water but then realized that this method of calculating snowfall was unreliable. Snow that falls in lower air temperatures is much fluffier, with far less water, than snow that falls when the temperature is higher. In fact, fluffy or powdery snow is 90 to 95 percent air! Ten inches (25 cm) of powdery snow melts down to as little as 0.1 inch (0.25 cm) of water, while the same amount of wet snow could equal as much as 4 inches (10 cm).

With a snow pillow, meteorologists measure snowfall by its weight.

An avalanche in
Switzerland

Beautiful but Deadly

Playing in the snow is one thing, but being trapped in it is quite another. Around the world, 150 people die every year in **avalanches**. In 1998, a record 26 people in the United States lost their lives to avalanches, or the "white death."

As temperatures rise, sections of hard mountain snowpack begin to melt, sending a wave of snow down upon unsuspecting skiers, climbers, and snowmobilers. A large avalanche in North America can release up to 300,000 cubic yards (230,000 cubic meters) of snow, which amounts to 20 football fields filled 10 feet (3 m) deep. Most deaths are caused by much smaller slides, however.

Scientists often close mountain recreational areas and trigger avalanches on purpose. With carefully placed explosives, loose snow can be brought down the slopes safely. This kind of avalanche control cuts the risk of a deadly slide when the mountain is packed with skiers.

People frequently get trapped not under snow but in it. In one storm in 1978, 150,000 people in the Midwest were without heat when power lines went down. Even more dangerous, 5,700 drivers were stuck in their cars along snowbound Ohio highways. These people faced the twin threats of **hypothermia**, a rapid loss of body heat, and **frostbite**, the loss of blood flow to extremities such as the nose, fingers, and toes.

Surviving White Death

Forty percent of the people caught in an avalanche suffocate because they do not know two simple tips: always try to "swim" to the top of the snow as the avalanche rolls over you, and punch the snow to form an air pocket so you can breathe until help arrives.

An entire landscape in Siberia is destroyed by acid rain.

Chapter Five

Dangerous Downpours

Rain helps clean the air by bringing down some of the gases, pollen, salt, and dust particles that naturally float in the atmosphere. When humans send pollutants into the sky, these chemicals also come down with the rain—often with deadly results. Gasoline and coal emissions from cars and factories spew large amounts of carbon dioxide (CO_2) and sulfur dioxide (SO_2) into the air. These pollutants change rain by creating drops with unnaturally high levels of acid.

Drip by drip, acid rain destroys valuable sculptures by eating away at the stone.

Carried around the globe by winds, **acid rain** harms plants, forests, and wildlife.

Rain forests, such as the Amazon in South America, are critical to our planet. They produce rain and life-giving oxygen and serve as a habitat for thousands of species of plants and animals. Scientists estimate that acid rain, along with over-logging and clear-cutting for farming, will completely wipe out our rain forests by the year 2100.

Acid rain can also damage stone by eating away at the calcium carbonate in limestone and marble. The Taj Mahal in

India, the Parthenon in Greece, and other historical monuments around the world are slowly being destroyed by acid rain. Without major restoration and clean-up efforts, architectural treasures will continue to disappear drip by drip.

Rivers of Sorrow

Rain usually soaks into the ground or travels into streams, lakes, and rivers, which then flow to the sea. When rain falls faster than the ground can absorb it, however, the **runoff** can flood croplands, destroy towns, and devastate lives. Flooding results from ice jams on rivers, the melting of mountain snowpacks, or long periods of moderate to heavy rain. A single major downpour that brings several inches of rain can cause a serious flood.

Flooding is one of the most destructive forces of nature on our planet. In the United States, floods kill more people than lightning, tornadoes, or hurricanes. **Monsoons**, strong winds that change direction with the seasons, are often to blame for floods in Africa, central South America, the southeastern United States, Australia, and Asia.

In the United States, more than one hundred lives are lost every year due to **flash floods**. These sudden floods occur when surges of water cause rivers to rise too quickly and overflow their banks. Ice jams, dam breaks, and heavy rain falling at 1 inch (2.5 cm) per hour or more can spark a flash flood. In the summer months, when the ground is dry, the sun-baked soil is often unable to absorb all the water in a downpour. The

Too Much or Too Little

Each year in India, winter monsoons blow away from the coastlines to create hot, dry **drought** conditions. In the summer, the winds reverse direction and bring in moist ocean air. The summer monsoons are considered a blessing because they bring much-needed rain for crops. The same winds are a curse, however, when they set into motion torrential rains and killer floods that can last for months. Between June and September of each year, India gets approximately 150 to 300 inches (380 to 760 cm) of rain. Sometimes weather patterns interfere with the monsoon breezes, however, and the rains never make it inland. Without this precious water, millions of acres of crops simply wither in the burning Sun, and thousands of people die of thirst and starvation.

runoff rushes downhill toward rivers and canyons and washes away chunks of dirt, rocks, trees, and anything else in its path.

A Mixed Blessing

One benefit of flooding is that it replenishes soil with valuable minerals and nutrients. Some of the world's richest croplands are located on flood plains. Stretching more than 2,300 miles (3,700 km) through the central United States, the Mississippi River has undergone thousands of years of flooding, erosion, and redeposition of nutrients. Wheat, soybeans, cotton, and other crops thrive in the fertile soils of the Mississippi Valley.

Sometimes the very floodwaters that deliver nutrients to soil are also the cause of major destruction. In 1927, heavy rains and a melting snowpack caused the Mississippi River to spill over her banks. More than 600,000 people were forced from their homes, and hundreds were killed as water submerged 26,000 square miles (67,000 square km) of farmland in seven states.

43

The Flood Control Act of 1928 led to the building of the longest system of **levees** and **reservoirs** in the world. The Mississippi River was even straightened in places to allow the water to flow more quickly. Confident that the longest river in the United States had at last been tamed, people moved back onto the flood plain.

In the summer of 1993, the illusion of safety was destroyed. In six months, 30 inches (75 cm) of rain fell in nine states, and

Major floods left seventy thousand residents of the Mississippi River flood plain homeless in 1993.

the Mississippi could no longer be contained. She broke through 80 percent of the levees designed to hold her, flooding millions of acres of farmland and wiping out whole towns. Seventy thousand people were left homeless, and the property damage was estimated at more than $20 billion.

Davenport, Iowa, was completely submerged by the 1993 rains.

River Dams

In August 1998, the Yangtze River caused the worst flooding China had seen in forty-four years. Three hundred million people—more than the entire U.S. population—were affected. In an effort to tame the Yangtze, which floods once about every ten years, the Chinese government began building the world's largest dam.

In 2006, when the Three Gorges Dam is completed, it will create a reservoir 400 miles (640 km) long. Sections of the river will be allowed to rise, and hundreds of old villages along the banks of the Yangtze will drown. More than one million people will have to relocate. Many fear losing not only their property, but also part of their rich culture, for many ancient temples, burial grounds, and historical structures will be forever lost.

The Three Gorges Dam, to be completed in 2006, will tame the Yangtze River in China.

Although the Yangtze is one of the world's most treacherous rivers, China's Huang He, or Yellow River, has taken the most lives. In the past hundred years, seven million people have died in the raging floodwaters that earned the river its nickname, China's Sorrow. The Yellow River flows higher than some of the villages on its banks. Thirty-foot (9-m) dikes are all that stand between the people and a disaster that could wash their towns off the map. It is hoped that construction of a modern dam will help control the river in the future.

Nature's Course and Ours

New advances in computer technology, better radar, and rain gauges are changing the way we view deadly storms and floods. Forecasters benefit from instruments such as **Doppler radar**, which sends out microwave pulses to pinpoint heavy rain. Doppler relays information about a storm's strength and direction to help meteorologists make earlier and more accurate forecasts. Scientists can now identify severe rainstorms about 12 to 24 hours before the first raindrop ever falls. This gives them the critical time they need to issue public flood warnings so that no one is caught by surprise.

The National Weather Service has also found success with an experimental river flood-forecasting program. The Advanced Hydrologic Prediction System (AHPS) disproves the old way of thinking that all rivers are alike. AHPS explores land use, soil, vegetation, and groundwater flows for each river. AHPS, along with other new technology, has increased

Getting the Drop on Rain

A new Doppler radar called S-Pol can peer into a storm to view the size and shape of raindrops. S-Pol can also spot hail, which is a major advance, since hail often fools standard radar (and forecasters) into thinking it is rain.

flood-forecasting accuracy by 40 percent. The United States has helped install AHPS in Egypt and China, the two countries hit hardest by floods.

If rain fell evenly over the planet, every place would get 34 inches (86 cm) of rain each year. Of course, it does not work quite that way. Ultimately, nature decides where, when, and how precipitation will fall, support living organisms, and shape climates around the globe. Imagine what Earth would be like without lush rain forests, sun-baked deserts, or deep, blue oceans. Then look to the skies and search the clouds for those first few precious drops of rain.

Glossary

acid rain—rain that has an abnormally high acid content due to increased levels of carbon dioxide and sulfur dioxide in the atmosphere

avalanche—the rapid downhill flow of large amounts of snow or ice dislodged from a mountain

blizzard—a heavy snowstorm or blowing snow, with winds above 35 miles (55 km) per hour, that lasts more than 3 hours

cloud—a visible formation of water droplets or ice crystals in the air

cloudbursts—heavy showers that produce large amounts of rain in a short period of time

cloud condensation nuclei (CCN)—tiny particles of dirt, dust, clay, salt, pollen, or pollutants onto which water vapor condenses to form clouds

condense—to change from a gas into a liquid

dewpoint—the temperature at which water turns from a gas into a liquid

Doppler radar—a weather instrument that sends out radio waves to track the intensity and movement of storms

drizzle—raindrops smaller than 0.02 inch (0.5 mm) across

drought—an extended period of time without significant rainfall

evaporate—to change from a liquid into a gas

flash flood—a rapid rise in water levels, often caused by heavy rainfall over a short amount of time

flurry—a snowfall that does not create measurable amounts of snow on the ground

freezing level—the altitude in the atmosphere at which the air temperature is 32° F (0° C), the freezing point of water

freezing rain—rain that freezes when it comes into contact with something on the ground, such as trees, roads, or power lines

frostbite—loss of blood flow to bodily extremities due to extremely low temperatures, with symptoms including numbness, tingling, and bluish-white skin

glaze—a layer of ice created by freezing rain

graupel—snowflakes that fall through a layer of supercooled water droplets and are coated with a hard layer of rime; also called soft hail

green sky effect—a glow cast by ice suspended within a thunderstorm; a potential sign of hail or a tornado

hail—balls of ice, created in warm thunderstorms, that grow larger as they are bounced back up into the atmosphere by strong winds

humidity—the amount of moisture in the air

hypothermia—a rapid loss of body heat due to exposure to low temperatures or prolonged wet conditions

ice storm—a severe winter storm in which freezing rain coats everything on the ground with a layer of glaze

levee—an earthen wall that diverts floodwaters from the towns and croplands near a river

monsoon—a seasonal wind that carries moist ocean air to dump heavy rains inland or moves dry air from overland

precipitation—any form of rain, ice, or snow that falls from a cloud

rain—drops of water that measure between 0.02 and 0.23 inch (0.5 and 6 mm) in diameter

rainbow—an arc of the six colors of sunlight, separated by raindrops through refraction and reflection

rain gauge—an instrument that collects rainfall

refract—to bend; in the case of rainbows, to separate the bands of color in light

reservoir—a man-made or natural lake that stores water and helps control the level of rivers

rime—supercooled water droplets that freeze on snow as it is falling and change the soft flakes into odd-shaped balls of ice

runoff—water that is not absorbed into the ground because either too much rain has fallen or the ground cannot absorb it fast enough

shower—rain or snow that falls, sometimes quite heavily, for a short period of time

sleet—ice pellets that form when rain or snow melts, then refreezes as it falls

snow—clusters of ice crystals that fall in temperatures below freezing and do not melt or refreeze on their way down

snow shower—a light snowfall in which flakes start and stop throughout the day and generally produce enough snow to measure

snowburst—a large amount of snow that falls during a short period of time

snowsquall—a brief but intense snowstorm that is often accompanied by strong winds

steady rain—rainfall that occurs over several hours or days with little or no break

supercooled water droplets—cloud droplets that do not freeze despite air temperatures that dip below the freezing point of water, 32° F (0° C)

thermal updrafts—pockets of moist air that, when heated by the Sun, rise to begin the cloud-formation process

trace—a rainfall amount totaling less than 0.01 in (0.25 mm), usually too little for a rain gauge to measure

virga—rain that evaporates before reaching the ground

water vapor—water in the form of an invisible gas

whiteout—a condition in which visibility is so low that it is difficult to distinguish between the ground and the sky

To Find Out More

Books

Allaby, Michael. *How the Weather Works*. London: Dorling Kindersley, 1995.

Baxter, Nicola. *Rain, Wind, and Storm*. Austin, TX: Raintree Steck-Vaughn, 1998.

Berger, Melvin, and Gilda Berger. *Can It Rain Cats and Dogs? Questions and Answers About Weather*. New York: Scholastic, 1999.

Christian, Spencer, and Antonia Felix. *Can It Really Rain Frogs? The World's Strangest Weather Events*. New York: John Wiley & Sons, 1997.

Kahl, Jonathan D. *Wet Weather: Rain Showers and Snowfall.* Minneapolis, MN: Lerner Publications Company, 1992.

Videos

Avalanche! NOVA, PBS, 1997, videocassette.

Flood: Overflowing the Banks. NOVA, PBS, 1997, videocassette.

Rain & Snow. Schlessinger Media, 1998, videocassette.

Organizations and Online Sites

The Discovery Channel
http://www.discovery.com
Search for nature videos and software; find your local weather forecast; learn about extreme weather; and hook up to live, interactive nature cameras.

National Oceanographic and Atmospheric Administration (NOAA)
Office of Public Affairs
U.S. Department of Commerce
14th Street & Constitution Avenue NW, Room 6013
Washington, DC 20230
(202) 482-6090
http://www.noaa.gov
The NOAA Web site features more than twelve thousand weather photos, 3-D weather images, and links to NOAA's

various affiliates. A special page for students explores hazardous weather, such as flash floods and blizzards, and provides safety tips. Link to the National Weather Service office located in your area for your local forecast.

National Snow and Ice Data Center
Campus Box 449
University of Colorado Institute for Research in Environmental Science
Boulder, CO 80309-0449
http://nsidc.org/
http://www.nsidc.colorado.edu
If you want to know about glaciers, ice caps, avalanches, blizzards, or anything involving ice and snow, you'll find it at the NSIDC Web site. Along with snow facts, winter storm-safety tips, and extreme weather events, you'll find a gallery with thousands of glacier photos dating back to the 1880s. Click on the Q & A section to find out what others are curious about or to post your own question for the experts.

NOVA Online
Public Broadcasting System
http://pbskids.org/
http://www.pbs.org/wgbh/nova
Search the *Savage Planet* and NOVA series for more on floods and dangerous weather. Also available are online games and activities for students.

Weather Underground
University of Michigan
http://groundhog.sprl.umich.edu/
One Sky, Many Voices is an interactive program that combines technology such as computer software and the Internet to educate students about weather and air quality. At *cirrus.sprl.umich.edu/wxnet* you can tap into more than eight hundred weather cameras across North America, find a temperature in your town or around the globe, and connect to one of the largest collections of weather links on the Web.

USA Today
http://www.usatoday.com/weather
Track approaching storms, learn more about winter weather, and find the forecast for your city at this easy-to-use site. The Weather Almanac offers rainfall and temperature statistics for cities around the world.

A Note on Sources

When researching weather, it is important not only to rely on a variety of sources but also to seek out the most up-to-date information available.

First, I consulted the National Oceanographic and Atmospheric Administration (NOAA), which has a local National Weather Service office in Seattle. NOAA's National Climatic Data Center in North Carolina, home to the world's largest active archive of weather data, provides the latest in rain, hail, and snow statistics. The Hydrologic Information Center and the National Snow and Ice Data Center offer more information on blizzards, avalanches, ice storms, and floods. Online sources such as the Weather Channel and *USA Today* feature weather graphics, safety tips, and additional facts.

I read as many reference and general books as possible, such as Walter Lyons's *The Handy Weather Answerbook*, Jack Williams's *The Weather Book*, and *The Old Farmer's Almanac*

Book of Weather and Natural Disasters. Narrowing the topic further, I looked to works such as *Floods,* by Michael Allaby, and *The Secret Language of Snow,* by Terry Tempest Williams and Ted Major. I also made a point to read as many books written for young readers on the topic as I could.

I kept an eye out for videos, news programs, and documentaries such as the Discovery Channel's *Storm Warning* series and PBS's *Savage Planet* and NOVA programs. Newspapers and magazines such as *Weatherwise* and *Scientific American* rounded out my research with the most current information on weather technology.

My travels have taken me to the lush temperate rain forest of Olympic National Park and the snowy peaks of Mount Baker, which in 1998–1999 set a new world's record for the most snowfall in a single season: 1,096 inches (2,783 cm).

Of course, being a native of the Pacific Northwest, I usually don't have to wait too long before raindrops tap on my own roof—thank goodness!

—*Trudi Strain Trueit*

Index

Numbers in *italics* indicate illustrations.

About the Author

As a weather forecaster for KREM (CBS) TV in Spokane, Washington, and KAPP TV (ABC) in Yakima, Trudi Strain Trueit has traveled to schools throughout the Pacific Northwest to share the world of weather with elementary and middle school students. She is the author of three other Watts Library Earth Science books: *Clouds, The Water Cycle,* and *Storm Chasers.*

An award-winning television news reporter, Trueit has contributed stories to ABC News, CBS News, CNN, and the Speedvision Channel. Trueit, who has a B.A. in broadcast journalism, is a freelance writer and journalist. She lives in Everett, Washington, with her husband, Bill.